_____

Presented to

_____

by

_____

on

You, special princess,
are a daughter of the King.

Princess

Tyndale House Publishers, Inc.
Carol Stream, Illinois

Stories  Real Bible Stories *of* God's Princesses

written by Carolyn Larsen

illustrated by Sergey Eliseev

Visit Tyndale's website for kids at www.tyndale.com/kids.

TYNDALE is a registered trademark of Tyndale House Publishers, Inc.

The Tyndale Kids logo is a trademark of Tyndale House Publishers, Inc.

Princess Stories: Real Bible Stories of God's Princesses

Copyright © 2011 by Carolyn Larsen. All rights reserved.

Cover and interior illustrations copyright © 2011 by Educational Publishing Concepts. All rights reserved.

Designed by Jacqueline L. Nuñez

Edited by Stephanie Voiland

Scripture quotations are taken from the *Holy Bible*, New Living Translation, copyright © 1996, 2004, 2007 by Tyndale House Foundation. Used by permission of Tyndale House Publishers, Inc., Carol Stream, Illinois 60188. All rights reserved.

For manufacturing information regarding this product, please call 1-800-323-9400.

Library of Congress Cataloging-in-Publication Data

Larsen, Carolyn, date.

    Princess stories : real Bible stories of God's princesses / written by Carolyn Larsen ; illustrated by Sergey Eliseev.

      p. cm.

    ISBN 978-1-4143-4811-7 (hc)

1. Women in the Bible--Meditations--Juvenile literature. 2. Girls--Prayers and devotions. I. Eliseev, Sergey, ill. II. Title.

    BS575.L365 2011

    242'.62--dc22

                               2011002353

Printed in China

17   16

7   6   5   4   3

Contents

Contents

Introduction

Have you ever wished you were a princess? Do you like to pretend that you are? Maybe your room is decorated in pink and your bed is built to look like a castle! Maybe you love to dress up in beautiful flowing dresses that make you look like Cinderella or Sleeping Beauty. Maybe your favorite movie is about a princess who faces some terrible danger but is rescued just in the knick of time. Or maybe you dream of living "happily ever after" someday, just like a princess.

Well, did you know that you *can* be a princess? It's true! You can be a real princess—God's princess! After all, the Bible says that God is a King—the King of everything in heaven and on earth. The Bible also says that God is our Father. So if you're the daughter of a King, that makes you . . . a real live princess!

We can read about some of God's other princesses in the Bible. Did you ever wonder who the bravest princess was? How about the most faithful princess? The kindest princess? Well, now is your chance to find out! Pretend you have a special mirror, and let's look into the Bible to learn about these real princesses of God.

Eve
The First Princess

Genesis 1:26–2:25

Mirror, mirror on the wall,
Who was the very first
princess of all?
A long time ago, before
your birth,
Eve was the very first
woman on earth.

Eve's Story

I am the first princess. I was the very first woman God created. Adam was the first man. God made him by using dirt from the ground and breathing God's own breath into him. God used one of Adam's ribs to make me, the first woman!

Adam and I lived in the Garden of Eden. It was a beautiful, happy place that God made for us. The Garden was full of gentle rivers, beautiful flowers, big trees, butterflies, swans, horses, and any other kind of animal you can think of.

God made sure we had everything we needed in the Garden. We knew how much he loved us. He gave us only one rule to obey. Life in the Garden was great . . . until I did something that messed everything up.

The rule God gave us was, "Do not eat the fruit of the tree in the center of the garden." We had plenty of other food to eat, so it wasn't like we needed the fruit. But I could not stay away from that tree. The tree was beautiful and the fruit looked delicious. One day I was standing by the tree when a snake crawled up. "Did God really tell you not to eat that fruit?" the snake asked.

"Yes," I said, "God told us we would die if we eat that fruit."

"You won't die. If you eat it, you will be just as smart as God," the snake said.

Everything the snake said made sense. I grabbed a piece of the fruit and took a big bite. It was so juicy! So sweet! I gave some to Adam, telling him, "You have to taste this!" Well, Adam tried it too, and that's when our perfect world fell apart.

As soon as we swallowed that fruit, we felt guilty. We knew we had done something wrong. That evening when God came to the Garden, we hid from him. But it isn't possible to hide from God! He knew where we were. He knew we'd eaten the fruit we were not supposed to eat. God was sad that we had disobeyed him, so we would have to leave the Garden of Eden.

But that's not the end of the story for me, the first princess. Even though Adam and I had disobeyed God . . . even though God was sad . . . even though he had to punish us . . . he still loved us. He would always be the King, and I would always be his daughter.

Bible Verse

If we confess our sins to him, he is faithful and just to forgive us our sins and to cleanse us from all wickedness.

1 John 1:9

Princess Ponderings

What was the one rule God gave to Adam and Eve?

When was a time you did something God didn't want you to do?

Read 1 John 1:9. What does this verse tell you about God's love and forgiveness?

Sarah
The Surprised Princess

Genesis 18:1-15; 21:1-7

Mirror, mirror on the wall,
Who was the most surprised
princess of all?
Sarah wanted a child but she
had none—
Then to her surprise God
gave her a son!

Sarah's Story

A long time ago God made a promise to my husband, Abraham. He promised that Abraham would have a big, big family. He said our family would have as many people as there are stars in the sky. That meant we would have lots of children and grandchildren and great-grandchildren, right? That was really exciting news!

5

But year after year went by, and we still didn't have any children. None. I was so sad. I wanted very much to be a mother. Abraham and I believed God's promise, but I was getting too old to have a baby. How could God keep his promise now?

One day three men who were walking across the desert stopped by our tent. It was a very hot day, so Abraham invited them to sit down in the shade to rest. He asked me to make some dinner for them. While I was cooking, I could hear the men and Abraham talking outside. I wasn't paying much attention until I heard one of the men say that by the same time next year Abraham and I would have a newborn baby! I laughed to myself. There was no way I could have a baby now—Abraham and I were both too old!

Here's the strange thing . . . I didn't say a word or laugh out loud, but the man turned to Abraham and asked, "Why is Sarah laughing? Don't you believe that God is big enough to make this happen? Don't you believe he can do anything?" I didn't know what to think. I wanted to believe that God could give us a baby. I wanted to believe that he would keep the promise he made to us long ago. It just didn't seem possible.

But soon I got the surprise of my life! I found out those messengers from God were right: I was really going to have a baby! Me . . . an old woman with an even older husband! God had kept his promise to us after all!

A few months later our son, Isaac, was born. We chose the name Isaac because it means "laughter." At first I laughed with doubt, but later I laughed with happiness. Isaac was our surprise from God!

Bible Verse

All the Lord's promises prove true.

Psalm 18:30

Princess Ponderings

Why did Sarah laugh when the man said she would have a baby?

Can you think of a time when you got a surprise?

Read Psalm 18:30. What does this verse teach you about why we can trust God?

Hagar
The Remembered Princess

Genesis 16:1-15; 21:1-21

Mirror, mirror on the wall,
Who was the most unforgotten
princess of all?
When Hagar was scared to be all
on her own,
God showed he remembered—
she wasn't alone!

Hagar's Story

You've heard Sarah's story, but now it's my turn
to tell my story. I knew Sarah well—in fact, I
was her servant. When God told Sarah and
Abraham to leave their home and go to
a new land, they went. And I went
with them. That's because
wherever the master goes,
the servant goes too.

At first, everything was going
fine in the new land. Abraham and
Sarah trusted God and followed him.
They tried to do what was right. Many
years ago, God had promised Abraham

and Sarah a son. But year after year passed, and there was still no baby for them.

Sarah started wondering if God was really going to keep his promise. So she decided to come up with her own plan to get a son. She told me that I should have a son for her. Pretty soon I found out I was going to have a baby. But even though this was Sarah's idea, she became really jealous of me.

Things got so tough for me that I ended up running away from Abraham and Sarah. I didn't get far when suddenly I was face-to-face with a big surprise! I was sitting down beside the road getting a drink, and there was an angel in front of me!

"Where are you going?" the angel asked me.

I told him I was running away, but the angel said I should go back to Sarah.

Then the angel said something I'll never forget. "The Lord has heard your crying. You will have a son, and his name will be Ishmael." Even though I felt all alone, God had not forgotten about me!

I went back to live with Sarah and Abraham. Sure enough, I did have a son, and I named him Ishmael. But he was not the son God had promised Abraham and Sarah. Years later when Sarah had her own son, Isaac, she got jealous again. But this time she wasn't just jealous of me. She was jealous of Ishmael, too. So I left again, and I took my son with me. I felt so alone.

Ishmael and I wandered around in the wilderness, and there was no water to drink. I was afraid my son and I were going to die. But just then I had another visit from an angel!

The angel said, "Don't be afraid! God has remembered you and your son." I opened my eyes, and right there in front of me was a well full of water! Even when I felt alone, I wasn't really alone. God had not forgotten me.

Bible Verse

I, the Lord, made you, and I will not forget you.

Isaiah 44:21

Princess Ponderings

How did Hagar know God had not forgotten her?

How can you tell God has not forgotten you?

Read Isaiah 44:21. What does this verse say about God remembering his children?

Rebekah
The Helpful Princess

Genesis 24:1-67

Mirror, mirror on the wall,
Who was the most helpful
princess of all?
When Rebekah took time
to help and to share,
She found that she was
an answer to prayer.

Rebekah's Story

My story is a love story—a beautiful love story. But it didn't start there. It started with a simple act of helping someone out.

Remember Isaac? He was the son of Abraham and Sarah. By the time Isaac was a grown man, Sarah had died and Abraham was very old. Abraham wanted his son to have a good wife who believed in

God. So Abraham sent his servant back to the town he grew up in to find a wife for Isaac.

This was a big responsibility for the servant. How would he know which woman would make a good wife for Isaac? But Abraham believed that God would send an angel ahead of the servant to prepare the right woman. The servant loaded ten camels with gifts and left for Abraham's hometown.

This is where I come into the story. The servant got to the town where my family lives. He stopped near a well and prayed, "God, please help me today. Show me which of the young women here is your choice to be Isaac's wife. I will ask a woman for a drink of water from this well. If she gives me a drink and also offers to get more water for my camels, I will know she is the one. Please help me, God."

About that time I came to the well to fill my water jug. Of course, I didn't know any of this was happening. I didn't know that the stranger who asked me for water was looking for a wife for his master's son. I didn't know about his prayer or about the sign he had asked God for. When the servant asked me for a drink, I gladly got some water for him. And after I gave him a drink, I offered to get more water for his camels. It turns out I was an answer to the servant's prayer!

When the camels finished drinking, the servant gave me gold bracelets. He also asked to meet my father, so I took him home with me. The servant explained that he had been sent to find a wife for Abraham's son. He told us all about his prayer and the way God had answered. Then he asked if I would go back to Canaan with him and marry Isaac. I was happy to become Isaac's wife, and he loved me very much. And it all started when I helped a man and his camels!

Bible Verse

Serve one another in love.

Galatians 5:13

Princess Ponderings

Why do you think Rebekah got water for the servant and his camels?

What are some things you do to help others?

Read Galatians 5:13. What does this verse tell us about being helpful to others?

Moses' Mom
The Protective Princess

Exodus 1:8–2:10

Mirror, mirror on the wall,
Who was the most protective
princess of all?
The story of Moses is exciting
to hear—
How his mother protected
him without any fear.

Moses' Mom's Story

The king of Egypt was afraid that the Israelites in his country would try to take over Egypt, so he made us slaves. He thought that one day the Israelite baby boys would grow up and fight back against the Egyptians. So he ordered that anyone who saw a young Israelite boy should throw him in the river.

17

About that time, I had a baby. He was a little boy named Moses. Something told me that this boy was special. Something told me that God had a job for him to do someday. I knew I couldn't let my son die. So for three months I hid him. I did everything I could to protect my son. But by the time he was three months old, he was getting too big and I could not hide him anymore. I was afraid someone would find him and take him from me.

So I came up with a plan. I went down to the river and picked some tall grass and wove it into a basket. Then I covered the outside of the basket so water wouldn't leak through. I put my baby son, Moses, in the basket and took it down to the river. I set the basket—with my little son in it—in the river and left it there. My daughter, Miriam, hid nearby to see what would happen. I trusted God to protect my son.

You'll never guess what happened! After a while an Egyptian princess came to the river with some of her servants. The princess noticed the little basket floating in the river and sent one of her servants to get it. Moses was crying when she opened it, and the princess felt sorry for him. She knew he was an Israelite boy, but she decided to take him home and treat him like her own son. Miriam raced down to the river and asked the princess if she needed someone to take care of the baby. The princess said yes, so Miriam ran and got me!

My son was saved, and one day he grew up to be a prince. God protected Moses, and he used me to protect him too.

Bible Verse

I am with you, and I will protect you wherever you go.

Genesis 28:15

Princess Ponderings

What did Moses' mom do to protect her son?

Can you think of a time when someone protected you? How about a time when you protected someone else?

Read Genesis 28:15. What does this verse say about how God protects us?

The Daughters of Z
The Teamwork Princesses

Numbers 27:1-11

Mirror, mirror on the wall,
Who were the best teamwork princesses of all?
They were five strong sisters, as close as could be.
They worked hard together, these daughters of Z.

The Daughters of Z's Story

The five of us are sisters, and we are good examples of how a team can work together. On our own, we might not be very strong. But when we stand together, we can do big things!

You see, there are no boys in our family. We don't have any brothers. And since our mom and dad died, there are just the five of us girls. Our father's name was Zelophehad. He was a good man. He listened to Moses, the leader

21

of our people. And he did not complain about God like many other people did.

Some time after our father died, our people, the Israelites, finally reached the land God had promised us. We had been wandering in the wilderness for a long time, and everyone was so happy to move in! Moses made plans about how to divide the land. He decided each man in the family would get part of a place to live. But since our father was dead and he had no sons, our family wasn't counted. That meant we would not get any land at all.

The five of us didn't think that was fair. We wanted a part of the land too, and we wanted our family to have a special place to call our own. So we came up with a plan and told Moses about it. We reminded him that our father had trusted the Lord and listened to Moses. We asked him to give us girls a part of the land. (It was a very brave request!)

Moses listened to us and asked God what to do. We were so happy when God said that we should be given the land! Then God said that from that point on, when a man who had no sons died, his daughters should get his part of the land. Now we had land of our own! And it all happened because we worked together . . . and because God heard our prayer.

Bible Verse

Two can stand back-to-back and conquer. Three are even better, for a triple-braided cord is not easily broken.

Ecclesiastes 4:12

Princess Ponderings

What plan did the daughters of Z tell Moses about?

Can you think of a time when you did something as part of a team?

Read Ecclesiastes 4:12. Why is it better to work as a team than to work by yourself?

Rahab
The Brave Princess

Joshua 2:1-24; 6:1-25

Mirror, mirror on the wall,
Who was the bravest princess of all?
Rahab was strong, and Rahab was brave.
She helped the people God told her to save.

Rahab's Story

This is my story about a tough choice I had to make. I'm not an Israelite myself, but I had heard a lot about the Israelites. I lived in Jericho, and my people were their enemies. I knew about the miracles God had done to free them from Egypt and to keep protecting them after that. I was scared of them, and I was amazed by their God.

One day two men came to my house looking for a place to hide. I saw that they were Israelites, and I let them in. Someone saw them and raced to tell the king that there were spies at my house. I knew the king would send soldiers to find them. I was scared of the soldiers but even more in awe of the God of the Israelites, so I took the spies up to the roof of my house and hid them.

The soldiers pounded on my door. "Where are those two spies?" they shouted.

"They were here," I said as bravely as I could. "But they left just before the city gates were closed for the night. If you hurry, maybe you can catch them!" The soldiers ran to search around the city gate, but the two men were still safely hidden on the roof of my house.

I went to talk with the spies. "Look, everyone in this city is afraid of you. We heard how God made a path for you to cross through the sea and how he saved you from your enemies. I believe that your God is very powerful! Since I've helped you, will you promise to protect my family and me when you come back to take over my city?"

"Yes, we will protect you," the spies said. "Just hang this red rope in your window so we'll know which house is yours."

That night I took the two men to the window and lowered them down to the ground outside. "Run for the hills!" I said. The men hid there for three days until the soldiers gave up looking for them. Then they headed home to tell the other Israelites what they had found out.

Later the Israelite army raced into Jericho to take over the city. My family and I huddled in my little house and waited to see if the spies would keep their promise. The red rope was still hanging in my window. Sure enough, even though everything around us was destroyed, my house and my family were kept safe! It was scary, but God helped me to be brave.

Bible Verse

Wait patiently for the Lord.
Be brave and courageous.

Psalm 27:14

Princess Ponderings

Why did Rahab decide to help the spies?

Have you ever been very brave? What happened?

Read Psalm 27:14. What does this verse tell us about why we can be brave?

Deborah
The Wise Princess

Judges 4:1–5:31

Mirror, mirror
on the wall,
Who was the wisest
princess of all?
If there were a contest
for who was most wise,
A judge named
Deborah would get
the prize.

Deborah's Story

Back in the days before Israel had a king to lead them, the country was ruled by judges like me. Whenever people needed advice, they would come to me. Day after day I sat under a palm tree while one person after another came and asked me to solve their problems. God gave me the wisdom to help them and show them what to do.

29

It was a tough job to be a judge in Israel. My people didn't really listen to good advice. They disobeyed God time after time! They would obey him for a while, and then they would start doing whatever they wanted. When things got tough, they'd beg God for help and promise to do the right thing. But before long they'd go back to disobeying again. By the time I became a judge, this had been going on for many years.

During the time I was a judge, Israel had been taken over by the king of Canaan. The leader of Canaan's army was an evil man named Sisera. He made life really hard for the Israelites for twenty years. Then one day God told me some exciting news: he would set his people, the Israelites, free from Sisera and his army! I gave this message to a soldier named Barak: "God says to gather 10,000 soldiers. He will bring Sisera to you, and you can defeat him. Israel will be free again!"

"I will get the soldiers and go to fight . . . but only if you go with me," Barak said. I told him I would join him, but if I did, the honor of defeating Sisera would go to a woman. So off we went to the battle.

Sisera heard that Barak had gathered an army, so he called for all his soldiers and all his chariots. They came to the river near Barak and the other Israelites. This was it! I told Barak to get ready to fight. God would go ahead of the Israelites, and he would give them victory.

When Barak's army attacked, God sent Sisera's army into a panic. In the middle of the battle, Sisera got scared and ran away. He hid in the tent of a woman named Jael. Jael told Sisera to lie down and rest. She even got him some milk to drink and covered him with a blanket. Sisera thought she was on his side, but she was really loyal to the Israelites. While he was fast asleep, Jael pounded a tent peg into his head. Everything turned out just as I had said—a woman got the honor of defeating Sisera!

Bible Verse

If you need wisdom,
ask our generous God,
and he will give it to you.

James 1:5

Princess Ponderings

How did Deborah show that she was wise?

Think of a time when you had a big decision to make. Did you choose the wise thing to do?

Read James 1:5. According to this verse, where does wisdom come from?

Naomi
The Role Model Princess

Ruth 1:1–4:22

Mirror, mirror on the wall,
Who was the best role model of all?
Of all the Bible princesses we've met,
Naomi stands out for the model she set.

Naomi's Story

My husband and I and our two sons lived in Bethlehem, and we were happy there. We had a nice home, and we liked being near our relatives and our friends. But then we had no rain for a long time, which meant no food would grow. So we had to move to a faraway country.

We packed up our things and moved to the land of Moab. We settled in and began to make friends . . . but then my husband died. I was so sad. But I was thankful to have my two sons with me. My boys grew up and got married, so now I also had two daughters-in-law! Then sadness came into my life again: both of my sons died. My heart was broken.

I decided it was time to go back home to my own city. I told my daughters-in-law that I was moving. I said they should go home to their families and look for new husbands. One daughter-in-law did just that. But the other one, Ruth, said she wanted to go to Judah with me. She said she wanted to go wherever I went, and she wanted to worship my God.

So I packed up my things again, and Ruth and I moved to Bethlehem. I was glad to have young Ruth with me. We were very poor, so Ruth went to the fields to pick up leftover grain for food. The

34

field she went to was owned by a man named Boaz, who was one of my relatives.

One day Boaz came by the field and noticed Ruth picking up the grain. He thought it was good that she was helping take care of me. So Boaz told his workers to leave some extra grain on the ground just for Ruth.

Ruth told me that Boaz was being very kind to her. I saw what a good man Boaz was, and I knew it would be a wonderful thing for Boaz and Ruth to get married. So I told Ruth what to do to make Boaz notice her. Ruth did exactly what I said. And sure enough, before long Ruth and Boaz were married. Ruth might say that I'm not just her mother-in-law—I'm also her role model!

Bible Verse

The godly offer good counsel;
they teach right from wrong.

Psalm 37:30

Princess Ponderings

Why do you think Ruth listened to Naomi and followed her advice?

Do you have any godly adults in your life who are role models for you? Are you a role model for anyone younger than you?

Read Psalm 37:30. What does this verse say about who you should get advice from?

Ruth
The Loyal Princess

Ruth 1:1–4:22

Mirror, mirror on the wall,
Who was the most loyal princess of all?
Ruth is the princess who was true blue.
She is a great example for you.

Ruth's Story

You already met my mother-in-law, Naomi, in the last story. But now it's my turn to tell my part of the story! Life was good in Moab at first. But things turned bad when Naomi's husband died. Then Naomi's sons died too. One of her sons was my husband. We were all heartbroken. Naomi had lost her husband and sons. I had lost my husband.

Now the only people left in the family were my mother-in-law,

Naomi; my sister-in-law, Orpah; and me. Naomi told us that she had decided to move back to Bethlehem, her hometown. She told us, "Girls, go back home and live with your families. Look for new husbands. You're still young. You can get married again." Orpah decided to go back to her family, just as Naomi said. But I wouldn't even think about it.

"Go on home, Ruth," Naomi said. "Your sister-in-law has turned around, and you should too."

But I knew deep in my heart that I should stay with Naomi. So I said, "Don't ask me to leave you. Wherever you go, I will go. Wherever you live, I will live. Your people will be my people. Your God will be my God. Nothing will keep us apart!" I guess she could tell I meant it, because she didn't say another word. We went on our journey to Bethlehem.

I was loyal to my mother-in-law, and God noticed that loyalty. Not long after we settled in Naomi's hometown, I married a good man named Boaz. We were so happy when we had a baby boy . . . and Naomi was thrilled to have a grandson!

Bible Verse

A friend is always loyal.

Proverbs 17:17

Princess Ponderings

How did Ruth show she was loyal to Naomi?

What are some ways you can show you're loyal to your friends or family?

Read Proverbs 17:17. What does this verse say about being loyal?

Hannah
The Praying Princess

1 Samuel 1:1-28

Mirror, mirror
on the wall,
Who was the most
prayerful princess
of all?
Hannah shows us just
how we can pray.
She cried out to God,
by night or by day.

Hannah's Story

Ever since I could remember, I wanted to be a mother. During the time I lived, it was very important for a woman to have children. Besides, I dreamed of having a baby to hold in my arms, to sing to, to teach, and to love. But year after year went by, and I didn't have any children. I loved my husband, Elkanah, and he tried his

41

best to comfort me. But I was still sad. I hoped that God would answer my prayers for a child.

Every year Elkanah and I went to the town of Shiloh to worship the Lord and make a special offering to him. One year, after wanting a baby for so long, I couldn't take it anymore. I broke down and cried. I trusted that God could give me a child, but it felt like he wasn't answering my prayers.

One night after dinner, when we were still at Shiloh, I went off by myself to pray. I was so upset that I just fell to the ground and cried. I was praying silently, not really saying words out loud. I begged God for a son. I promised God that if he would give me a son, I would give him back to God. I would let my son be God's servant for his whole life. I was praying with all my heart.

The old priest, Eli, saw me crying and moving my lips but not making any sound. He didn't know what was happening. I told him that I was pleading with God to give me a son. "Go in peace!" he said. "May God give you what you asked for."

Sure enough, God answered my prayer! About a year later, my son Samuel was born. And I kept my promise to God. When Samuel was old enough, I took him back to the priest, Eli, so he could serve God for the rest of his life.

Bible Verse

Don't worry about anything;
instead, pray about everything.

Philippians 4:6

Princess Ponderings

What did Hannah ask God for in her prayer?

Say a prayer right now, thanking God for one thing and asking him for one thing.

Read Philippians 4:6. Based on this verse, what kinds of things should we pray about?

Abigail
The Peaceful Princess

1 Samuel 25:2-42

Mirror, mirror on the wall,
Who was the most peaceful
princess of all?
A woman named Abigail,
peaceful yet strong—
She helped other people so
they'd get along.

Abigail's Story

My husband Nabal was a very rich man, but he also had a terrible temper. This got him in trouble more times than I can count. Sometimes when he lost his temper, I had to do everything I could to make peace. And that's exactly what I did one day when David and his soldiers came to our house.

We had all heard of David and his mighty army. In fact, David and his soldiers had treated our shepherds and

45

their flocks kindly in the past. Now David and his soldiers were running away from King Saul, who was trying to kill them. David's men asked my husband Nabal if he'd share some food with them. But my husband said, "No way! Why should I give anything to David and his friends?" When David's men reported what Nabal said, David got angry. He ordered his soldiers to grab their swords. He was ready to fight!

Now I didn't know any of this was happening until one of our servants came to tell me. Pretty soon David and 400 armed men would be at my house, ready to fight! I knew Nabal would never apologize, so I sprang into action.

I had my servants gather a bunch of food, including 200 loaves of bread, lamb meat, 100 bunches of raisins, and 200 cakes. Then I had them load all the food onto donkeys and head out to meet David. I got on my own donkey and followed them. When we met David on the path, I stopped in front of him. Then I said, "I'm sorry, sir. My husband has a bad temper. Please accept these gifts we're giving you. You are a good man, and you wouldn't want to do anything foolish in your anger. I know the Lord will take care of you and make you the leader of Israel. And when that happens, please remember my kindness to you."

David was grateful that I made peace and saved him from getting into a battle with my husband and our servants. David accepted my gifts, and he and his men went on their way. And there is another interesting part of my story: David kept his promise to remember me when he became king of Israel. After my husband Nabal died, David asked me to marry him . . . and I became queen!

Bible Verse

God blesses those who work for peace,
for they will be called the children of God.

Matthew 5:9

Princess Ponderings

What did Abigail do to make peace?

What are some things you can do to help people get along?

Read Matthew 5:9. What does this verse say about people who make peace?

The Widow
of Zarephath
The Trusting Princess

1 Kings 17:8-24

Mirror, mirror on the wall,
Who was the most trusting
princess of all?
This woman was down to her
very last meal,
But still she trusted that her
God was real!

The Widow of Zarephath's Story

When I first met Elijah, I was picking up sticks to make a fire. But this wasn't just any fire. It was a fire to make the last meal for my son and me. We were down to our last little bit of flour and oil. I was getting ready to bake our last loaf of bread.

Ever since my husband had died, we had been poor. But it had never been this bad. On that day I was sure we were going to starve after we ate our last meal. It was one thing to trust God when life is easy. But could I trust even when it looked like there was no hope?

As I was picking up sticks for the fire, the prophet Elijah came into the yard. "Would you please bring me a cup of water?" he asked. Of course, I was happy to do that for him. But as I went toward the house, he asked me to bring him a piece of bread, too.

"Sir, I can't do that," I said. I told him I had only a handful of flour and a little bit of oil—just enough to make a last loaf of bread. After that my son and I would starve.

"Don't worry," Elijah said. "Go inside and bake a small loaf of bread for me. Then bake another loaf for you and your son. I promise you there will always be enough food for you and your boy." I believed this man because he was a servant of God. And I trusted that God would take care of us. So I did what he said. Elijah was right! My son and I had plenty of food for many days. No matter how much flour and oil I used, there was always more in the jar for the next time! It was truly a miracle.

A while later, after Elijah had gone on to another place, my son got very sick. He kept getting worse and worse, until one day he died. I sent someone to get Elijah. I didn't know what else to do. This was another moment when it was hard to trust. "Why did you save my son a while ago only to let him die now?" I asked Elijah. But I still believed God could do another miracle.

"Give me the boy," Elijah said. He took my son upstairs and laid him on the bed. I heard him pray to God, "Please, Lord, bring this boy back to life!" Then I heard two sets of footsteps coming down the stairs. My son was alive! I learned that God can always be trusted.

Bible Verse

In him our hearts rejoice, for we trust in his holy name.

Psalm 33:21

Princess Ponderings

How did the woman in this story show she trusted God?

Can you think of a time you trusted God?

Read Psalm 33:21. What can we learn from this verse about trust?

The Shunammite Woman
The Sharing Princess

2 Kings 4:8-37

Mirror, mirror on the wall,
Who was the most sharing
princess of all?
When the prophet Elisha
needed to stay somewhere,
The woman from Shunem was
happy to share.

The Shunammite Woman's Story

I had great respect for God's prophet Elisha. He traveled from town to town doing God's work. He often came through our town of Shunem, and I always invited him for dinner. One night after Elisha had eaten dinner with my husband and me, I had an idea. "Why don't we build a room up on our roof for Elisha?" I asked my husband. "We can put a

53

bed, a table, a chair, and a little lamp in it. Then he will always have a place to stay when he comes to Shunem." So that's what we did! I was really happy to share with Elisha.

Elisha was happy to have the room too. He asked what he could do for me. I couldn't think of anything I needed, though. I had enough money, and my family took good care of me. But Elisha's servant noticed there was one thing I didn't have: a son. So Elisha told me that by the same time next year, I would have a little boy. I had always wanted a son! I could hardly believe it, and I told Elisha not to get my hopes up. But the prophet was right. By the next year, I did have a son. I was so happy!

A couple of years later, my son was out in the field with his dad. All of a sudden his head started to hurt. One of the servants brought my son to me. I held him and tried to help him feel better. But he kept getting worse and worse. Soon he was dead. I was so sad. I couldn't believe God would give me a son and then let him be taken away from me. I took my boy up to the little room we had built for Elisha and laid him on the bed. Then I got on a donkey and rode to the town where Elisha was staying. "I told you not to get my hopes up about having a son!" I cried.

Elisha told his servant to go to my house. "No!" I cried. "I will not leave here unless you go with me and help my son!" Elisha didn't argue. He came with me right away. He went to his room and prayed to God. Before I knew it, my son was alive again!

It's true that I shared things with Elisha, like food and a place to stay. But God gave me even more. He gave me a son . . . and he gave him back to me after he died!

Bible Verse

God will generously provide all you need. Then you will always have everything you need and plenty left over to share with others.

2 Corinthians 9:8

Princess Ponderings

Why do you think this woman gave Elisha food and a room to stay in?

What is one thing you can share with someone else this week?

Read 2 Corinthians 9:8. What does this verse tell you about sharing?

Naaman's Servant
The Faithful Princess

2 Kings 5:1-19

Mirror, mirror on the wall,
Who was the most faithful
princess of all?
Naaman's servant girl was not
very old,
But she had a faith that was
surprisingly bold!

Naaman's Servant's Story

For me, being a kid hasn't always been easy. My country, Israel, was invaded by one of our enemies, and they took some of us as servants. It was pretty scary because I was taken away from my family and sent to live with another family. I worked as a maid for a man named Naaman and his wife.

One morning I heard some terrible news. Naaman had a skin disease called leprosy. Since there weren't hospitals and doctors during the time I lived, this disease was really scary. No one knew of a way to cure it.

I knew that a servant girl is supposed to stay quiet and only speak when spoken to. But I had to say something, because I knew someone who could help Naaman. "I wish he would go see the prophet Elisha," I said. "He is a man of God, and he could heal Naaman." So Naaman's wife told Naaman what I had said.

Naaman was willing to do anything to be healthy again. So he took some of his servants and went to Israel to see Elisha. But when he got there, Elisha never came out of the house. He sent a servant out instead. The servant told Naaman to go to the Jordan River and wash himself seven times.

Naaman was angry that the prophet sent someone else with the message instead of coming out himself. He stomped away and said he was just going to go home. But his servant stopped him. "What do you have to lose?" the servant asked. "Try washing in the Jordan and see if it helps you." So Naaman washed himself in the river seven times. When he came up the last time, he was healed!

I was faithful to keep believing in God, even after I was taken away from my family and my country. And I was faithful in serving Naaman and his family. But God was the most faithful of all—he is the only one who could heal someone who is sick!

Bible Verse

You must remain faithful
to what you have been taught
from the beginning.

1 John 2:24

Princess Ponderings

How did Naaman's servant girl show she was faithful to God and to Naaman's family?

What is something you can do to show your faithfulness to God?

Read 1 John 2:24. What does this verse say about staying true to what you have been taught about Jesus?

Huldah
The Teaching Princess

2 Kings 22:8–23:25

Mirror, mirror on the wall,
Who was the best teaching
princess of all?
Huldah was wise and shared
what she knew.
She loved to serve God and
teach others too.

Huldah's Story

When you think of prophets
from the Old Testament, maybe
men like Isaiah or Daniel or
Jonah come to mind. But did
you know that there were
also prophets in the Bible
who were women? I was one
of them!

I lived during the time of King Josiah. Josiah
was only eight years old when he became the
king of Judah. At the time he was king, things
were not going well in our country. The
people had not been obeying God's laws,

61

and the Temple was in bad shape. When Josiah had been king for 18 years, he decided to do something about that. So he hired workers to fix up the Temple and make it beautiful again.

As they started repairing the Temple, the high priest found the Book of the Law! This was the book where God's laws were written down. It was his special message to the people, and it had been missing for years. When King Josiah heard about the Book of the Law, he sat down right away and had someone read the whole book to him. When the king heard what was written in the book, he was very sad. Now he knew that he and the whole country had been disobeying God.

That's where I come into the story. The high priest came to me for advice since he knew I was a prophet. I listened carefully, and then I said, "The Lord has spoken through this book. Go tell the king that

God says he will punish the city because the people stopped obeying him. But also tell the king that God knows he is sorry for not following God's laws. So you will not see this punishment during your lifetime, King Josiah."

I was happy to be able to teach King Josiah about how God looks at the heart. It was a good chance to teach him that God wants us to obey, but he is also willing to forgive.

King Josiah listened to every word of my message. He made laws so the people would start obeying God. He tore down the altars that had been built to false gods. He began celebrating the special holidays God wanted his people to celebrate. Josiah was a good king with a good heart. He listened to my teaching, and he learned what God wanted him to do.

Bible Verse

Anyone who listens to my teaching and follows it is wise, like a person who builds a house on solid rock.

Matthew 7:24

Princess Ponderings

What did Huldah teach King Josiah about God?

Who has taught you about God? Who can you teach so they will know more about God?

Read Matthew 7:24. What does this verse say about following God's teaching?

Esther
The Daring Princess

Esther 1:1–8:17

Mirror, mirror on the wall,
Who was the most daring
princess of all?
When God had a daring,
impossible task,
He knew young Esther was
the right one to ask.

Esther's Story

I never set out to be daring. But my people were in trouble, and I was the only one who could help them. And I believed God would be with me!

My parents died when I was a little girl, and I went to live with my relative Mordecai. My people, the Israelites, had been living in Persia for many years after being taken over in a fierce battle. One day the king of Persia decided to hold a contest. He wanted to find the most beautiful girl in the kingdom to be his

65

new queen. I was asked to enter the contest. I never dreamed I would win, but believe it or not, I became the new queen of Persia!

Life in the palace was great until one of the king's officials started causing trouble. This man's name was Haman. He worked in the government and had a pretty important job. The king ordered everyone to bow down to Haman each time he walked by. Most people did, but my relative Mordecai refused. He said he would only bow to God.

Haman got very mad at Mordecai. He decided to do whatever it took to get rid of Mordecai. But even that wasn't enough! No, he wanted to get rid of all the Israelites! Haman tricked the king into signing a law. This law would give him the power to kill all the Israelites. What Haman didn't know—and what the king didn't know either—was that I was an Israelite!

As soon as Mordecai heard about Haman's plan, he came to me and said that I had to do something. "What can I do?" I asked.

"Maybe you became queen just for this time," he said. "Maybe God has chosen you to save our people." That was scary, because if I went to the king without being invited, he could have me killed! I thought about it, and then I sent a message asking our people to pray. I would talk to the king, I decided. And if I died for it . . . well, I would die.

I invited the king and Haman to a special dinner. My plan was to talk to them and find some way to save my people. The dinner went well, and I invited both men back for a second dinner. Meanwhile, Haman was only getting angrier about Mordecai and the rest of the Israelites.

After the second dinner, the king offered to give me anything—even up to half of his kingdom. "I want only one thing," I answered. "Please save me and my people. Haman is planning to kill all the Israelites. I am an Israelite too. That means I will die along with my people." The king was upset that Haman had tricked him. He ordered that Haman get the punishment he had been planning for Mordecai.

My people were saved! You could say I was daring, but that's only because God gave me the strength in the first place.

Bible Verse

Be strong and courageous! Do not be afraid or discouraged.
For the Lord your God is with you wherever you go.

Joshua 1:9

Princess Ponderings

What did Esther do that was really daring?

Can you think of a time when you or someone you know did something daring? What happened?

Read Joshua 1:9. What does this verse teach us about being daring?

Elizabeth
The Honored Princess

Luke 1:5-80

Mirror, mirror on the wall,
Who was the most honored
princess of all?
When God had some very
exciting news,
Elizabeth was just the woman
to choose.

Elizabeth's Story

Some people are honored with special awards or prizes. But I got the biggest honor of all: God chose me to have a part in his plan when his Son, Jesus, was born. Here's my story.

My husband, Zechariah, was a priest in the Temple. We wanted to be parents, but we were old by now, and we had never been able to have children. One day when my husband was doing his job as a priest, he was chosen to go into the inner room of the Temple.

69

While Zechariah was there, God sent an angel to him with a special message. The angel said that soon we would have our very own baby! The angel said that we should name our son John. He also promised that when this boy grew up, he would point many people to God. My husband was shocked. He asked the angel how this could happen since we were so old. The angel told Zechariah that because he didn't believe the message, he wouldn't be able to talk at all until our son was born.

The angel was right! Soon I was expecting our baby. I was so happy to think that at last I would have a child. I didn't know it, but just a few months after I became pregnant, my young relative Mary was also visited by an angel. She was told that she would have a baby. But this would not be just any baby. Mary's baby would be Jesus, God's own Son!

Mary came to visit me when we were both waiting for our babies to be born. As soon as I heard Mary's voice, the baby inside me jumped! I had never felt anything like that before. I knew that Mary's baby must be very special. "Mary," I said, "you are blessed above all other women! I am honored that the mother of my Lord would choose to visit me." Somehow I knew the truth about Mary's baby before she even said a word.

When our son was born, our friends suggested that we name him after his father. But I remembered what the angel had told my husband. So I said, "No, his name will be John." Everyone turned to Zechariah to see what he thought. My husband agreed with me. He wanted to obey God and do what the angel had said. He got something to write with and put down this message: "His name is John." Right at that moment, his voice returned and he could speak again! We praised God for our dear little son, John.

As John grew up, we found out that the angel was right again. In his short life, John showed many people who Jesus was. I'm so glad God chose to honor me so I could be John's mother . . . and the first one to recognize Jesus, even before he was born.

Bible Verse

The Father will honor anyone
who serves me.

John 12:26

Princess Ponderings

Why do you think God chose Elizabeth to be the mother of John?

One of the ways God honors people is by giving them a special job or a chance to do something for him. What is something special God might want you to do?

Read John 12:26. Who does God give honor to?

Mary, Jesus' Mom
The Obedient Princess

Matthew 1:18-24; Luke 1:26-56; 2:1-20

Mirror, mirror on the wall,
Who was the most obedient
princess of all?
When God had a job for her,
Mary said yes.
That's the kind of heart that
God loves to bless!

Mary's Story

Obeying means that sometimes you have to do things that aren't easy. That was true for me. I was engaged to marry a man named Joseph. But before Joseph and I were married, the angel Gabriel came to see me.

"God is happy with you," Gabriel said. Then he told me that God had chosen me to have a baby who would be God's own Son . . . the Messiah! All my life I had heard about the

Messiah, who would come to save his people. I never for a minute dreamed that I would be his mother. I asked the angel how any of this could happen since I wasn't married yet.

Gabriel told me that God would be the father of this baby. He told me that my relative Elizabeth was about to have a baby too. I couldn't wait to talk with her. If anyone could understand about God doing something amazing like this, it would be Elizabeth.

I thought about everything the angel had said. I was amazed that God would choose me to be the mother of his Son. I thought about how good God is and how he was keeping his promise to send someone to save his people. Even though I was scared, my heart wanted to obey God. So I said, "I am the Lord's servant. I will do whatever he wants."

Later Joseph told me that an angel had visited him, too. The angel told him about my baby. This boy would be God's own Son, the angel said. Joseph should name him Jesus. The angel also told Joseph to go ahead with his plan to marry me.

After a few months, Joseph and I went to Bethlehem to be counted by the government. While we were there, Jesus was born. We couldn't find any place to stay because the town was so full of visitors. We finally ended up in a stable, surrounded by animals. And that's where my baby was born.

Later that night, some shepherds came to visit Baby Jesus. An angel had told them that the Savior, Jesus, had been born! After they saw Jesus, they left praising God. I thanked God for letting me be a part of his plan to save the world through his Son. I was so glad I said yes!

Bible Verse

If you love me, obey my commandments.

John 14:15

Princess Ponderings

Why do you think Mary was happy to obey God and say yes to him?

When is it hard for you to obey? When is it easy to obey?

Read John 14:15. What can you learn from this verse about obeying?

Anna
The Patient Princess

Luke 2:25-38

Mirror, mirror on the wall,
Who was the most patient
princess of all?
A woman named Anna
knew how to wait.
She trusted that God will
never be late!

Anna's Story

You might wonder if I'm too
old to be a princess. But my
story is proof that no one is
too old for the King to use!
I got married when I was
young. But not many
years after that, my
husband died. I was
all alone. I wasn't a wife
or a mom. But I still found
important things to do
for God!

I spent all my time in the Temple, day and night. I served God and prayed to him with all my heart. I was waiting patiently for the Messiah to come—the one God had promised. I didn't know when that day would be, but I trusted that God's timing was just right.

One day, when I was 84, I heard a lot of noise in the Temple. I went to see what was going on. An old man named Simeon was holding a little baby. He was full of joy and was praising God. Simeon knew that this baby, Jesus, was the Messiah! He was the one I had been waiting for so long!

When I saw Jesus, I was filled with joy too. I praised God for sending his Son to rescue his people. Afterward I told everyone I met about this child . . . God's gift to us. He was worth the wait!

Bible Verse

Rejoice in our confident hope.
Be patient in trouble,
and keep on praying.

Romans 12:12

Princess Ponderings

How do you think Anna was able to be patient for so many years?

Can you think of times you've been patient?

Read Romans 12:12. What does this verse say about being patient?

Mirror, mirror on the wall,
Who was the most forgiven
princess of all?
The forgiven woman met
Jesus at the well,
Then she ran to find others
she wanted to tell.

The Woman
at the Well's Story

I was just about the least likely person to be a princess! For one thing, my people, the Samaritans, were looked down on by the Israelites. And even my own people looked down on me. I had made some bad choices in my life, and before I met Jesus, I wasn't exactly a good role model. But then one day I met Jesus, and my life was never the same again.

At the time I lived, people didn't have running water to wash dishes or take a bath. We had to go to a well and get water out of it each day. Most women went to the well early in the morning or in the evening, when it was cool outside. But as for me, well, I usually went during the hottest part of the day. That was when no one else was there. Then no one would be able to make fun of me or be mean to me.

One day when I went to the well, I saw a man sitting on a rock nearby. I could tell he was an Israelite. *Good*, I thought. *At least he won't talk to me.* Usually Israelites didn't want anything to do with us Samaritans. So I just ignored him and went to get water from the well.

I put my bucket down into the well. As I pulled it up, the man said, "Could I have a drink, please?"

"You're asking *me* for a drink? I can't believe you are even speaking to me," I said.

"If you knew who I am, you would know what an amazing gift God wants to give you. You would be asking me for that gift—the gift of living water," he answered.

I had no idea what he was talking about. He didn't even have a bucket to get water out of the well!

"After you drink the water from this well, you will get thirsty again," Jesus told me. "But the water I can give you takes thirst away forever."

Wow, that sounded good to me. So I said, "Can I please have some of that water?"

Then Jesus told me all kinds of things about my life—things he wouldn't have been able to know from just meeting me! I could tell this was someone special.

"I am the Messiah," Jesus said. "One day people from all over the world will know about salvation. Someday people will worship God with all their hearts, in the right way." I believed at that very moment that he was the Messiah! Only he could save me and forgive me.

I ran to town to tell everyone to come to the well. I wanted them to meet the Messiah too!

Bible Verse

Though your sins are like scarlet, I will make them as white as snow. Though they are red like crimson, I will make them as white as wool.

Isaiah 1:18

Princess Ponderings

What is the "living water" Jesus talked about in this story?

Who do you think needs forgiveness? How can we be forgiven?

Read Isaiah 1:18. What does this verse say about God's forgiveness?

Jairus's Daughter
The Blessed Princess

Luke 8:40-56

Mirror, mirror on the wall,
Who was the most blessed
princess of all?
Jesus did something you
might not have guessed:
He raised a girl from the
dead—now talk about
blessed!

Jairus's Daughter's Story

I'm just 12 years old, but I am a princess too! Most of my story happened when I was lying in bed sick, but it's still a pretty amazing story. Once you hear about it, I think you'll see I was a really blessed girl!

My dad was an important leader in my town's place of worship. I was his only daughter, and he loved me very much. When I got sick, he became worried. I kept getting sicker and sicker, and he didn't know what to do.

Then my dad heard that the teacher named Jesus was in a nearby town. Dad had heard stories about Jesus helping blind people see again and healing sick people. Dad hoped that Jesus could help me, too. So he hurried to the town where Jesus was teaching.

When Dad got to the place where Jesus was, it was easy to spot him. There were huge crowds all around him. It was hard for Jesus to even walk down the road because of all the people around him. But my dad wasn't about to let those crowds stop him. He fell down at Jesus' feet. He told Jesus about me and said I was very sick. He asked Jesus to come to our house and heal me.

Jesus started walking toward our home with Dad. But before they'd gotten very far, a woman grabbed the bottom of Jesus' robe. Jesus stopped right there in the middle of the street to talk to this woman and heal her. Just then one of Dad's servants ran up to him. He said, "Leave the Teacher alone. Your daughter has already died. Don't bother Jesus anymore." My dad sadly turned away to come home.

But Jesus had heard what the servant said. "Don't be afraid," Jesus told my dad. "Just have faith, and your daughter will be healed." I'm sure

Dad didn't understand exactly what Jesus was talking about, but he headed home with Jesus anyway. When they got there, they found me lying on a bed inside the house. All our friends and family knew I was dead, and they were crying. But Jesus said something really surprising: he told everyone to stop crying. He said I wasn't really dead! They thought he was crazy.

Jesus brought three of his friends and my mom and dad into the room with him. And this is the amazing thing that happened next: Jesus took my hand and said very loudly, "Little girl, get up!" And right away I got out of bed! Jesus had brought me back to life. "I think this girl needs a snack," Jesus said to my parents.

I have a second chance at life now! I know that I am very, very blessed.

Bible Verse

Blessed are those who trust in the Lord
and have made the Lord their hope and confidence.

Jeremiah 17:7

Princess Ponderings

Why did Jairus's daughter feel blessed?

What are some of the ways God blesses you every day?

Read Jeremiah 17:7. What does this verse say about who God blesses?

Mary, Martha's Sister
The Listening Princess

Luke 10:38-42

Mirror, mirror on the wall,
Who was the most listening
princess of all?
Mary knew what was best;
nothing got in her way.
She wanted to listen to what
Jesus had to say.

Mary's Story

I lived in a small town called Bethany, not far
from Jerusalem, with my sister, Martha, and my
brother, Lazarus. We
were good friends with
Jesus, and whenever he
was in town, he would come by to
visit. Sometimes he'd eat meals with us,
and sometimes he'd stay with us for a while.

I loved it when Jesus came to our house. I loved talking
with him, but mostly I loved listening to him. Jesus

89

taught me about God and what it meant to live for him. He taught like no one I had ever heard before. I couldn't think of anywhere I'd rather be than right beside him, learning from him.

One day Jesus and his friends stopped by our house for dinner. They were on their way to Jerusalem, and our house was right on the way. Jesus had 12 special followers, so that meant there was a big group of people to feed. In those days we didn't have microwaves . . . and we couldn't just order pizza! My sister, Martha, was scurrying around the kitchen chopping and cooking and getting dinner ready. There was a lot of work to be done, but I didn't go in and help her. I sat down on the floor right at Jesus' feet and listened as he began talking. I didn't want to miss a word!

But Martha was upset. She went right up to Jesus. "It's not fair!" she said. "I'm working hard to get dinner ready for you and your friends. But Mary is just sitting here doing nothing. I shouldn't have to do all this by myself! Tell her to get up and help me!"

Jesus looked at Martha with love in his eyes. "Martha, Martha, you are so worried about all these details. But Mary has figured out what is really important—learning more about me! I'm not going to take that away from her."

Jesus taught us both a big important lesson that day: Sometimes listening is more important than doing. Sometimes we need to stop being so busy. There are times we just need to sit at Jesus' feet and learn from him.

Bible Verse

Anyone who belongs to God listens gladly to the words of God.

John 8:47

Princess Ponderings

Why was Mary happy to listen to Jesus?

Is it hard for you to listen to your parents and other adults? What does it mean to listen to God?

Read John 8:47. What does this verse say about listening to God?

The Widow in the Temple
The Giving Princess

Luke 21:1-4

Mirror, mirror on the wall,
Who was the most giving
princess of all?
This generous widow gave
all that she had.
She gave from her heart, and
that made her glad.

The Temple Widow's Story

If you had seen me in the Temple, you might not have even noticed me. I didn't have nice clothes, and I didn't have a lot of money. I didn't have a big-time job, and I didn't have important friends. My husband died a while ago, and I've been poor ever since.

If you went to the Temple, you probably would have noticed the rich people there—the ones who made a big deal of putting their money in the offering box. They liked to show off how good they were and how generous they were. But their hearts weren't always in the right place when they were giving.

I never had much to give. But I loved to give whatever I did have. God had been so good and generous to me. So whenever I could give my money away, it was a way to thank him. It was a way to give back to him. I didn't have a lot left for things like food and clothes. But I knew God would take care of me.

One day I went to the Temple like I always did. I waited until all the rich people had put their money in the offering box. I wasn't doing this for show, so I just waited until the crowd died down. Then I quietly went up and put in my two small coins.

But this time I noticed someone standing back watching me. The teacher Jesus and some of his followers were there. He was teaching them, as he often did.

After the rich men proudly put in their big offerings and I put in my small amount, Jesus had something to say. "This poor woman has given more than everyone else!" he told his followers. "They have given out of their wealth. This woman has given everything she has."

I was as surprised as anyone to hear Jesus say that! I guess it's true—he really does care most about our hearts! I am glad God allows us to give back, no matter how much or how little we have.

Bible Verse

God loves a person who gives cheerfully.

2 Corinthians 9:7

Princess Ponderings

Why did Jesus say the woman in the Temple had given more than anyone else?

How can you give with a glad heart?

Read 2 Corinthians 9:8. What does this verse tell us about being generous?

Mary Magdalene
The Changed Princess

Matthew 27:45-61; Luke 8:1-3; John 19:1–20:18

Mirror, mirror on the wall,
Who is the most changed
princess of all?
Mary Magdalene had a hard
life, it's true,
But when she met Jesus, he
made her brand new!

Mary Magdalene's Story

I was one of the first people to witness the greatest miracle in history. That was a high point of my life. But my story didn't start there. If you had met me earlier in my life, you never would have believed God would choose me to play a special part in his plans. I guess you could say I'm proof that God really does change lives!

When I first met Jesus, I was a complete mess. There were evil spirits that controlled me. They made my life miserable—they

97

ruined my relationships with other people and with God. But when I met Jesus, my life changed forever! He cast out the evil spirits and made me a new person. After that I followed Jesus wherever he went. I was part of a small group of women who traveled with Jesus and gave money to support him and his disciples.

But after a while, things started getting tense. The religious leaders got really angry at Jesus. One awful night they had Jesus arrested and decided he should be killed—even though he hadn't done anything wrong! When they hung Jesus on the cross, many of his other followers left. Maybe they were scared or just didn't know what to do. But I wasn't going anywhere. I stayed right there with Jesus, near the cross.

I stayed there until he died, and I watched as he was buried. On Sunday morning, as soon as I could, I rushed to the tomb where they'd placed Jesus' body. I was expecting to find him there dead. But it was the strangest thing—the big stone that covered the opening of the tomb was rolled back. The tomb was open! I peeked inside, but Jesus' body wasn't there. He was gone!

I was so upset. I went outside and tried to figure out what might have happened. I saw a man standing nearby, and I thought he might be the gardener. I asked him if he had taken Jesus somewhere.

"Mary," he said.

All at once I knew it was Jesus! He was alive!

Jesus had told us many times that he would be raised from the dead, but I didn't really understand it before. And now here I was, the first person to see Jesus when he came back to life. His resurrection was the biggest miracle in history!

I ran as fast as I could to tell Jesus' other friends what I'd found out. Jesus was alive, and he chose me—a changed woman—to share the good news!

Bible Verse

Anyone who belongs to Christ has become a new person.
The old life is gone; a new life has begun!

2 Corinthians 5:17

Princess Ponderings

How was Mary Magdalene changed?

How has Jesus changed your life?

Read 2 Corinthians 5:17. What does this verse teach you about Jesus' power to change us?

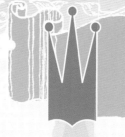

Tabitha
The Kind Princess

Acts 9:36-42

Mirror, mirror on the wall,
Who was the kindest
princess of all?
If you're looking around for
a princess who's kind,
Tabitha may be the kindest
you'll find!

Tabitha's Story

I lived in the time just after Jesus died and was brought back to life again. I was one of the believers in the first Christian church. I loved Jesus, and one of the biggest ways I showed that was by being kind to others.

One of my favorite things in life was to help people. For as long as I could remember, I had always had a soft spot in my heart for people who were poor or lonely or facing problems. I wanted to do whatever I could to help out.

I especially liked helping women whose husbands had died. In the time I lived, women couldn't work to make money, so many of these women were poor. They didn't have much money for food and clothes. That made me sad, and I decided I wanted to do something for them. So I started making clothes and coats for them. It made me feel good to see their smiles and know that I had done something kind for them.

But then one day I got sick. My friends did their best to take care of me, but nothing seemed to help. I just kept getting sicker and ended up dying. Believe it or not, though, that's not the end of the story!

My friends heard that Peter was in a town nearby. They knew that he was God's servant. God had helped him do some amazing miracles. So they asked him to come to my hometown and see if there was anything he could do.

When Peter got here, my friends brought him to the room where they had put my body. They stood around crying and telling him about my kindness to them. They showed him the clothes and coats that I had sewn for them. They begged him to do something.

Peter asked all my friends to leave the room. He knelt down beside my dead body and prayed to God for help. Then he turned to me and simply said, "Get up, Tabitha!" It was a miracle! Life rushed back into my body, and I opened my eyes. I was alive! Peter called my friends back into the room and showed them that I was not dead anymore.

There's something I've learned about kindness over the years: once it gets going, a little bit seems to catch on and spread!

Bible Verse

Do to others whatever you would like them to do to you.

Matthew 7:12

Princess Ponderings

What things did Tabitha do that showed her kindness?

What are some things you can do to show kindness to someone else?

Read Matthew 7:12. What does this verse say about how we should treat others?

Lydia
The Welcoming Princess

Acts 16:11-15

Mirror, mirror on the wall,
Who was the most welcoming
princess of all?
If anyone needed a warm
place to rest,
Lydia welcomed them in as
her guest.

Lydia's Story

The day started out as an ordinary
Saturday. I went down to the river
with some friends in the morning,
and I wasn't expecting anything
unusual to happen. But that day
I met some people who would
change my life forever.

Before I tell you the rest of my
story, here's a little bit about
me. I have a job selling cloth
for people to make dresses
and other clothes. In the time I
lived, most people wore simple
colors like white and brown and

105

tan. That's because colored cloth cost a lot more money. But the cloth I sold was special—it was purple. My business was doing well, and a lot of wealthy people bought cloth from me.

I lived pretty far away from where Jesus had lived—all the way across the ocean. I didn't know much about him. But I did love God. I worshiped him and tried my best to do what was right.

Then on that Saturday, there were some visitors from Israel in my city. A man named Paul and his friends came down to the river where some women and I were meeting. These men told me all about Jesus—how he lived a perfect life, how he died on the cross, and how he was raised to life again. They told me God loved me and wanted to forgive me. I believed that what they said was true! I wanted to follow Jesus too.

That day I got baptized, right there in the river. So did everyone else in my family!

I was so happy to have this new relationship with God. I wanted to do everything I could to show God how much I loved him. So I turned to Paul and his friends. "Please come and stay in my home," I told them. "I'll give you meals to eat and a place to sleep." I wanted to show I cared about them. I couldn't think of a better way to do that than to have them as guests in my home!

Bible Verse

When God's people are in need, be ready to help them. Always be eager to practice hospitality.

Romans 12:13

Princess Ponderings

Why do you think Lydia welcomed Paul and his friends into her home?

Who can you and your parents invite into your home for a meal or a visit?

Read Romans 12:13. Why do you think God wants us to be welcoming to other people?

Priscilla
The Respectful Princess

Acts 18:1-28

Mirror, mirror on the wall,
Who was the most respectful
princess of all?
Priscilla was wise and knew
how to teach.
She showed respect in her
actions and speech.

Priscilla's Story

My husband, Aquila, and I loved teaching
people about God. Our job was to make tents
to sell—that's how we made money. But the
thing we cared most about doing was telling
people about Jesus. We lived in Greece, but we
weren't born there. We used to live in Italy until
the ruler there made us and all the other Israelites leave
the country. So we made our home in a big city called
Corinth and started our business there.

While we were in Corinth, we met a man named Paul.
Paul made tents for a living, just like we did. He loved
God too, and he taught people about God every chance
he got. When he came to Corinth, he stayed at our

home. We learned so much from him about Jesus and about serving God and knowing him better.

After Paul had been in Corinth for about a year and a half, he decided it was time to go on to a new place. There were other people who needed to hear about Jesus. So my husband and I got on a boat and left Corinth with him. Aquila and I stopped in a city called Ephesus, right along the seashore. Paul kept on sailing and went to visit churches in other cities.

When we were in Ephesus, we met a man named Apollos. He was an amazing teacher, and he knew the Bible very well. Apollos loved to teach others about God. He was very excited about his faith, and he wanted other people to know God too. But as we listened to him teach, we found out he didn't know everything about what it means to be a Christian. We knew he needed to learn the whole story about Jesus so he could help other people follow Christ.

We knew we had to talk to Apollos. But we didn't want to make him feel embarrassed in front of other people. We wanted to teach him the truth in a respectful way. So my husband and I pulled Apollos aside and spoke with him in private, when there were no crowds around. We told him about all that Jesus had done. Apollos was very glad we taught him these things. And we were glad to have him as our friend!

Bible Verse

Respect everyone, and love your Christian brothers and sisters.

1 Peter 2:17

Princess Ponderings

How were Priscilla and her husband respectful of Apollos?

How can you be respectful of others' feelings?

Read 1 Peter 2:17. What does this verse say about who we should treat with respect?

Lois and Eunice
The Family Princesses

2 Timothy 1:3-5

Mirror, mirror on the wall,
Who were the best family
princesses of all?
Lois and Eunice raised a
wise young man
Who faithfully served as
part of God's plan.

Lois and Eunice's Story

You won't find much about us in the Bible, but we still had an important job behind the scenes! Besides, even if you haven't heard about us, you have probably heard about our boy, Timothy. There are even two books in the New Testament named after him!

These books are actually letters written to Timothy

113

by Paul, an important leader in the early Christian church. Timothy was Paul's helper, and he traveled around with him to help churches get started. Timothy was one of the youngest followers of Christ who went with Paul. He learned a lot from Paul, and Paul even treated him like his own son.

But back to where we fit into the story. Lois was Timothy's grandmother, and Eunice was his mother. We did all the things loving parents and grandparents do for their children—we made a good, safe home for him, and we did all we could to help him grow up healthy and strong. But there was something that was even more important to us. We wanted Timothy to know God and love him with his whole heart.

One time Paul said that Timothy had "genuine faith." He saw how the faith we had continued strong in Timothy. That's the nicest thing anybody could say about us. We know that the best gift we could give our boy is faith in God. We believed in God and in his Son, Jesus, and we did our best to live out that faith every day. Then, from the time Timothy was just a boy, we taught him everything we could about following Jesus.

Timothy grew up to be a fine young man, and he spent his life sharing the good news about Jesus with others. Paul gave Timothy some difficult jobs to do. He asked him to stand strong against people who were teaching things that weren't true. Timothy was also sent to encourage new believers in their faith.

We were very proud of Timothy and the work he did with Paul. But most of all we were thankful that he had a strong faith in Jesus his whole life, starting from a young age. We were glad that God let us—his mom and his grandma—teach him from the very beginning!

Bible Verse

Direct your children onto the right path,
and when they are older, they will not leave it.

Proverbs 22:6

Princess Ponderings

What did Timothy's grandmother and mother teach him?

What are some things your parents or grandparents have taught you about God?

Read Proverbs 22:6. Why is it good to learn about God while you're young?

You
The Special Princess

Psalm 139:1-24

Mirror, mirror on the wall,
Who is the most special
princess of all?
You, special princess, are a
daughter of the King.
You're more precious to
him than any other thing!

Your Story

Do you have a favorite story about a princess from the Bible? Do you want to be loyal like Ruth or wise like Deborah or daring like Esther? Maybe there is a princess you want to be like when you grow up. But guess what? You don't have to just dream about being as special as these women in the Bible. God has chosen you and made you special, just the way you are. And you don't have to wait until you grow up to do important things for God. He wants to use you right now, princess!

117

Psalm 139 tells you just how much your heavenly Father, the King, loves you. You are more special to him than anything else. He knows everything about you. He sees you when you're sitting down or standing up. He sees you when you're home and when you're away from home. He knows everything you do, everything you say, and everything you think. No matter where you go, he will go with you. And it makes him happy to take care of you and bless you.

Before you were even born, God knew you. He made every part of you—from the top of your head all the way down to your toes. He created you to be special, and there is no one else like you. He knew everything that would happen to you even before the first day of your life.

You are always on God's mind. No one could even count all the times he's thinking about you! He stays close to you all the time. He loves you so much, and he wants you to live with him forever. You are his princess, and he will never stop loving you!

Bible Verse

How precious are your thoughts about me, O God.
They cannot be numbered!

Psalm 139:17

Princess Ponderings

What is something amazing you've learned about what God thinks about you?

Have you asked Jesus into your heart so you can be a real princess—a daughter of the King? If you haven't, talk with a parent or teacher to begin your princess journey!

Read Psalm 139:17. How often does God think about you?